Where Animals Live

Mountain Animals

By Katie Buckley

I see snow leopards in
the mountains.

I see bald eagles in
the mountains.

3

4   I see cougars in the mountains.

I see wolves in the mountains.

I see elk in the mountains.

I see marmots in the mountains.

I see mountain goats in
the mountains.

I see yaks in the mountains.

I see bears in the mountains.

I see alpacas in the mountains.

I see moose in the mountains.

I see ibexes in the mountains.

Word List

vocabulary words

mountain	cougars	bears
mountains	wolves	alpacas
snow	elk	moose
leopards	marmots	ibexes
bald	goats	
eagles	yaks	

I see snow leopards in the mountains.

I see bald eagles in the mountains.

I see cougars in the mountains.

I see wolves in the mountains.

I see elk in the mountains.

I see marmots in the mountains.

I see mountain goats in the mountains.

I see yaks in the mountains.

I see bears in the mountains.

I see alpacas in the mountains.

I see moose in the mountains.

I see ibexes in the mountains.

CHERRY BLOSSOM PRESS

Published in the United States of America by Cherry Lake Publishing Group
Ann Arbor, Michigan
www.cherrylakepublishing.com

Photo Credits: © Jack Bell Photography/Shutterstock, cover; © Leonid Andronov/Shutterstock, title page; © Asmakhan992/Shutterstock, 2; © FloridaStock/Shutterstock, 3; © Evgeniyqw/ Shutterstock, 4; © Volodymyr Burdiak/Shutterstock, 5; © Alfie Photography/Shutterstock, 6; © Astrid Gast/Shutterstock, 7; © Joshua Schutz/Shutterstock, 8; © CEW/Shutterstock, 9; © ArCaLu/Shutterstock, 10; © Lisa Stelzel/Shutterstock, 11; © Michael Liggett/Shutterstock, 12; © Alexander Ingerman/Shutterstock, 13; © FloridaStock/Shutterstock, 14

Note from publisher: Websites change regularly, and their future contents are outside of our control. Supervise children when conducting any recommended online searches for extended learning opportunities.

Cherry Blossom Press is an imprint of Cherry Lake Publishing Group.

Library of Congress Cataloging-in-Publication Data

Names: Buckley, Katie (Children's author), author.
Title: Mountain animals / written by Katie Buckley.
Description: Ann Arbor, Michigan : Cherry Blossom Press, [2024] | Series: Where animals live | Audience: Grades K-1 | Summary: "Mountain Animals showcases animals found in a mountainous environment, including animals like alpacas and snow leopards. Uses the Whole Language approach to literacy, combining sight words and repetition. Simple text makes reading these books easy and fun. Bold, colorful photographs that align directly with the text help readers with comprehension"— Provided by publisher.
Identifiers: LCCN 2023035092 | ISBN 9781668937594 (paperback) | ISBN 9781668939970 (ebook) | ISBN 9781668941324 (pdf)
Subjects: LCSH: Mountain animals—Juvenile literature. | Mountain ecology—Juvenile literature.
Classification: LCC QL113 .B83 2024 | DDC 577.5/3—dc23/eng/20230901
LC record available at https://lccn.loc.gov/2023035092

Printed in the United States of America

Katie Buckley grew up in Michigan and continues to call the Mitten her home. When she's not writing and editing, you'll find her gardening, playing music, and spending time with her dog, Scout. She has always loved books and animals, so she's a big fan of this series.